D1097482

"Golf today is all about understanding the importance of the fundamentals. Your knowledge of these fundamentals will drastically and immediately improve your game. Bill, whom I believe is one of the top young coaches in the country, has done amazing research in this area using tour players as the model. I believe this book will help you better understand how and why you need to pay attention in this area. I hope you enjoy the book as much as I did. Play better golf with Bill Schmedes!"

—Gary Gilchrist
Golf Digest's "Top 50 Best Teachers in America" and
Golf Magazine's "Top 100 Teachers in America"

"I have had the distinguished pleasure to work with Bill and many of his golfers over the years. Frankly, Bill is one of the top coaches I have spent time around! His extraordinary dedication and efforts in developing golfers of all ages and abilities is second to none. It is obvious from Bill's resume that he can teach and instruct golf from a technical standpoint. It is, however, a whole other skill to coach and develop players on the mental, emotional, and strategic aspects of golf. Bill is able to do all of these, which is why he's become so successful. Bill's book, The 5 Tour Fundamentals of Golf, *is no different. Bill has taken his knowledge and research and put it down on paper.* The 5 Tour Fundamentals of Golf *is a fantastic read, and I encourage golfers of all ages and abilities to pick this book up yesterday!"*

—Dr. Dan Vosgerichian
Mental Coach

"Over the span of my career, I have been fortunate to be involved in the training and mentoring of countless young golf coaches and instructors both in the U.S. and abroad, many of

whom now populate today's "Top 50 Teachers" and "Top 100 Instructors" lists or lead the golf industry in their various areas of expertise. It is my pleasure to say that few, if any, have matched or even met the promise I see for a bright future in coaching and teaching as Bill Schmedes. Bill has all the characteristics that I look for in a great coach/instructor. He is caring, conscientious, honest, hardworking, loyal, and dedicated. Bill has a "sharp eye" and a very solid (and continuously growing) knowledge base in every aspect of the game of golf. He also possesses a very inquisitive mind and is always willing and passionate to learn and grow even more for the betterment of himself and his students. This book truly shows the passion Bill has for finding the answers in the hope of helping others improve their golf games!"

—Patti McGowan
Golf Digest's "Best Teachers in State" (Florida) and
Golf Magazine's "Top 100 Teachers in America"

The 5 TOUR FUNDAMENTALS of GOLF

BILL SCHMEDES III

Cover and text design by Beth Farrell
Cover and text layout by John Evanston

Sea Script Company
Seattle, Washington

ISBN: 978-0-9907631-2-3

First Printing April 2015

Printed in the United States

Sea Script
SEA SCRIPT COMPANY
www.seascriptcompany.com
info@seascriptcompany.com
206.390.6628

TABLE OF CONTENTS

FOREWORD

Patti McGowan

Over the span of my career, it has been my great pleasure and good fortune to be involved in the training and/or mentoring of countless young golf coaches and instructors both in the U.S. and abroad, many of whom now populate today's "Top 50 Teachers" and "Top 100 Instructors" lists. These professionals lead the golf industry in their various areas of expertise. A short list of some of these coaches and instructors that you may readily recognize includes, but are not limited to: Nick Bradley, Gary Gilchrist, Sean Hogan, Don Hurter, Brian Mogg, Andrew Nicholson, Andrew Park, Andrew Rice, Don Sargent, Kevin Smeltz, and David Whelan.

I take great joy in observing the number of worldwide victories that have been achieved by professional golfers with the help of the countless coaches that I have been fortunate to have had a part in training and mentoring early in their teaching careers. That joy is quadrupled when I pause to reflect on the realization that for every one tour victory achieved with the help of one of the coaches I've worked with at some point, there are probably hundreds, if not thousands, of golfers out there enjoying a better golf game as a result of the good work done by these professionals.

"Back in the day" at Lake Nona, while working with David Leadbetter, we enjoyed a special time of unprecedented growth in the golf industry, especially in golf instruction and training. One fond memory I have is of many of us crowding in front of a small mirror in a unisex/shared locker room in the old DLGA trailer, hurriedly putting on our sunscreen in preparation for our very busy days. At that time, it was like the Wall Street of the golf business. We almost always headed off in our separate directions greeting each other with the phrase: "We're off to make golf a better game, and to make golf games better." And, indeed, so many of us really have!

It's exciting to anticipate that the number of improved golfers may be exponentially expanded by the work of yet another up and coming "Top Teacher," Bill Schmedes. Bill has all the characteristics that I look for and have observed in great coaches and instructors over the years. Bill is caring, conscientious, honest, hardworking, loyal, and dedicated. He has a "sharp eye" and a very solid and continuously growing knowledge base in every aspect of the game of golf. He also possesses a very inquisitive mind, and is always eager and passionate to learn and grow even more for the betterment of himself and his students. His tireless and thoughtful study and research of the over 180 tour players' swings used in this book is evidence of his passion for continuing to maximize his effectiveness in helping all levels of golfers improve as quickly as possible. His efforts have resulted in five easily identifiable and understandable common swing characteristics shared by today's top touring professionals.

I am confident that you will find all of the concepts discussed in Bill's work to be intriguing. Many reflect an admirable ability I've noticed in many gifted coaches: To see things from a different perspective than the average person. Chapter One on Grip Sync is one example of that. There is no doubt in my mind that any golfer that is able to model and duplicate these positions will indeed improve their ball striking. Eventually, even if all other parts of the game remain the same, better ball striking will eventually result in better control of the golf ball. Over time, this will no doubt result in lower scores. Without question, every golfer can improve their ball striking and ultimately their scoring by emulating The 5 Tour Fundamentals of Golf that you are about to discover in this book.

Carefully read and study Bill's work, practice the tests and drills in Chapter 6, and prepare to play some of the best golf of your life!

INTRODUCTION

Bill Schmedes III

"Five researched and proven golf fundamentals displayed by the best golfers in the world for you to use in your game!"

For decades, the traditional golf fundamentals have been the Holy Grail of golf instruction. There has always been a specific way players were told to address the ball, grip the club, move the body, and swing the club with regard to swing plane. These fundamentals have been written about in books by many of the greats in golf: *Ben Hogan's Five Lessons: The Modern Fundamentals of Golf*, *Bobby Jones On Golf*, Jack Nicklaus's *Golf My Way*, and *Harvey Penick's Little Red Book: Lessons And Teachings From A Lifetime In Golf*. I learned from reading these classic books as a young instructor and found that many of the instructors I mentored under were teaching the same information. As the years passed, I have taken many of golfs' original fundamentals and applied them to golfers with the understanding that each player is an individual and you have to teach them the game that way. There is not a one-size-fits-all model out there for every player.

I have been fortunate to have grown up in the golf industry. Truthfully, I have never had a job outside of the golf industry!

During that time, I met several people I consider influential in helping to groom me into the professional that I am today. I've learned many life lessons both playing the game and working for specific professionals or golf instructors as I've moved through the ranks. After college, I was lucky enough to get my first position in the industry at a resort facility on Cape Cod, Massachusetts. This resort had the busiest golf academy in the area, where I quickly discovered my passion for teaching golf and helping others. From that time on, I have been very lucky to have mentored and studied under many of today's great golf coaches. Two of the most influential have been Patti McGowan and Gary Gilchrist.

Patti McGowan was David Leadbetter's Director of Training for over ten years, training many of today's Top 100 and Top 50 golf coaches, including Gary Gilchrist. She has been recognized on countless lists by *Golf Digest* and *Golf Magazine* as being one of the top golf coaches in the world, and has worked with players like Nick Faldo and Nick Price when those players were in their prime.

I'm fortunate to have also worked under Gary Gilchrist. He spent many years working under David Leadbetter and ran the IMG Academy for him. He then became Director of Instruction at the International Junior Golf Academy in South Carolina, where he coached a handful of juniors that would eventually play on the PGA and LPGA tours. His passion for junior golf eventually lead him to start his own academy in Orlando, Florida. The Gary Gilchrist Golf Academy is one of the biggest junior golf academies in the world!

Learning under Gary in Orlando has been a special time for me and my teaching development. I've been lucky enough to work with many of the better juniors in the world while also assisting

Gary with his tour players on both the PGA and LPGA tours. These players have won Major titles and various other events all over the world.

Some of Gary's most impressive work was developing Michelle Wie into the player she is today. The same is true for Yani Tseng who became the number one player in the world under Gary, and won five Major Championships on the LPGA Tour.

During my time at GGGA, I've been lucky enough to work with top PGA Tour players Charles Howell III, Arjun Atwal, and Morgan Hoffmann. On the LPGA Tour, I've worked with Yani Tseng, Shanshan Feng, Sandra Gal, Karen Stupples, Alison Walshe, and Vicky Hurst. These players have provided great insight into what it takes to become a successful touring professional, which is one of the reasons I researched tour fundamentals and wrote this book.

Over the years I've studied hundreds of golf swings of touring professionals on all of the major tours. I have also had the opportunity to both work and watch some of these players first-hand. They're special because they all have certain intangibles that have allowed them to become very successful world class players. When you walk the range at an event and watch these professionals, you find all sorts of different grips, postures, alignments, spine tilts, and widths of stance. And that's before they even begin the swing! Going down the line, you see different swing planes, clubface orientations, body movements, ball flights, and trajectories.

My goal for this book was to research a large database of touring professionals and try to find what these players all did alike in their golf swings. You would think the best players in the world would be close to what many consider technically sound when it comes to the original fundamentals of golf, and how the club and body should move to help the club stay on plane. This isn't necessarily true!

As I began my research, I found certain absolutes that all the professionals were applying to their golf swings. They were not necessarily the original fundamentals of golf as I learned them growing up, but *as I continued to see player after player doing the same things, I figured I may be on to something here!*

After researching over 180 swings, I was able to come up with absolutes that each player applied. I want to share this information with the public to help golfers improve at a faster clip. My research helped me find five absolutes that each player applied in their game. I call these "The 5 Tour Fundamentals of Golf." The 5 Tour Fundamentals of Golf are easily achieved by anyone no matter the age, ability, or gender. If you apply these fundamentals to your game, I guarantee you will lower your score!

You will not hear me talk a lot about some of the things that most instructional books detail, such as posture and alignments at address. Not all players are physically able to put themselves in the same posture, as I've seen from tour players, and alignments change based on the player's desired ball flight. I won't get overly detailed about the path and plane of the club in the backswing. I don't do this because it's not a fundamental found in the best players in the world. I *will* tell you that specific fundamentals, if done correctly, can and will help you with regard to the path and plane of the club, especially in the downswing.

Each chapter will outline a fundamental that will give you a clear understanding of what you need to do to lower your scores. Following the chapters, there will be drills to help you do two things: test and implement. Some chapters will need you to test yourself to see your current abilities. Once you understand your current methods, we can implement changes by using the correct drill for you.

These are The 5 Tour Fundamentals of Golf I have researched and found to be effective:

1. GRIP SYNC
2. TOUR FOUNDATION
3. TOUR TRANSITION
4. TOUR DELIVERANCE
5. TOUR STRETCH

The 5 TOUR FUNDAMENTALS of GOLF

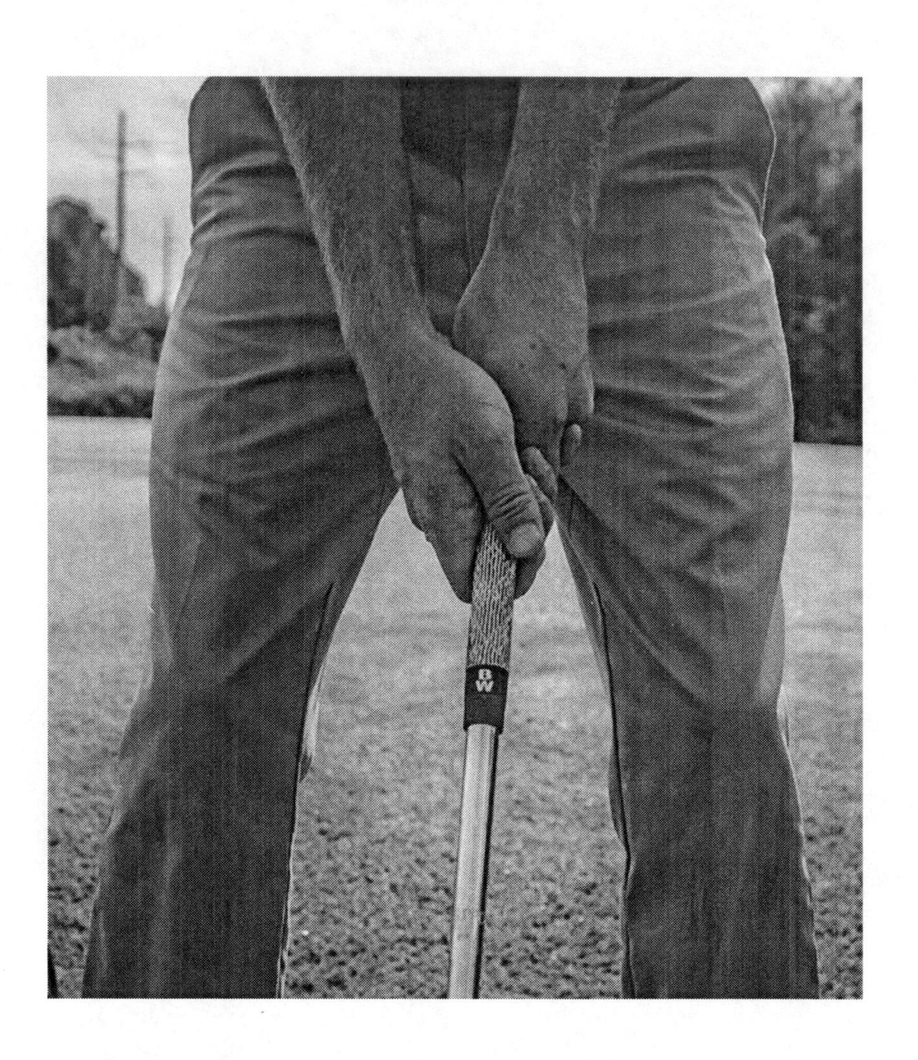
B
W

1 GRIP SYNC

The grip in golf instruction is arguably the most important fundamental talked about when it comes to golf's primary fundamentals.

Any golf instruction book I've ever read has a chapter solely on how to place one's hands on the club. This book is no different, but what will be different is how I describe the correct grip compared to most golf books.

The grip is responsible for the clubface and has an effect on how the player hinges the club in the backswing and then releases the club after impact. So yes, the correct grip is very important for the player to have. *But what is the correct grip?*

I grew up learning golf's fundamentals as did most players that began playing at an early age. I learned that I should hold the club with what's considered a "neutral" grip, meaning the top hand is placed with the palm pad on top of the handle with the golfer seeing two knuckles, placing the crease that is created between the thumb and the index finger pointing towards the trail ear. The low hand then follows suit by using the thumb pad to hide the top hand thumb. If this is done properly, the crease between thumb and index finger should point between the trail ear and the shoulder. This was the grip we were all taught as junior golfers because it would supposedly give us the best chance to square the clubface up at impact. Were my instructors correct? As the great Harvey Penick would say, "That depends."

I've done research and read research showing the importance of understanding the body in the golf swing and its effect on the club face. Every golfer will have different rotational abilities. Players will naturally have low, standard, or higher rotational abilities. These rotational abilities effect the amount of turn the body segment will have. It's very important to understand this when talking about how one should grip the golf club because of its effect on the clubface. If a player doesn't know their rotational ability, they are only guessing when it comes to how they grip the golf club. I call this "Grip Sync" (Fundamental No. 1).

I often see instructors attempting to slow or increase a player's rotational speed. In my experience, this is one of the most difficult changes to make due to each player having different body makeups. Without a rigorous golf-specific workout plan, these players will have a very difficult time changing what the body does naturally. In fact, research has shown that even if a player does a golf-specific workout, it can still take between six months to a year for their bodies to cooperate. Some specialists actually lean towards one to two years!

The top players I've had the opportunity to work with or have researched have all done a fantastic job of either consciously or subconsciously syncing their grips with their bodies and their desired ball flight. I've learned to distinguish the correct grip by understanding the rotational ability each player currently has. I watch the amount of rotation the body has at impact and this rotation determines the proper grip for that player:

- A player with higher rotational ability opens the hips up more through impact compared to their shoulders, which causes their belt buckle to face the target. This means the clubface will stay open for a longer period of time leading up to impact. This player needs to have a stronger grip. Strong grip players include: David Duval, Paul Azinger, Zach Johnson, Fred Couples, Dustin Johnson, Jason Duffner, John Daly, Tommy Gainey, Yani Tseng, Boo Weekley, Carl Pettersson, Matt Kuchar.

- A player with less rotational ability will have hips with less turn compared to their shoulders. This player can be classified as more of an "arms swinger" and will naturally want to close the clubface at impact. This player will need a slightly weak grip. Weak grip players include: Ernie Els, Greg Norman, Corey Pavin, Johnson Wagner, Will MacKenzie, Brandon Grace, Brandon De Jonge, Inbee Park, Graham Delaet, Paul Casey, Luke Donald, Jason Gore.

- Finally, the player that has what I consider standard rotational ability will be able to match both hips and shoulders up at impact. The player's upper and lower body will come close to a 45-degree angle. This player is best suited to grip the club as I was taught—with a neutral grip. Neutral grip players include: Keegan Bradley,

Tiger Woods, Phil Mickelson, Jason Day, Webb Simpson, Robert Allenby, Adam Scott, Paula Creamer.

I naturally had a higher rotational ability so I really needed a stronger grip than the one that was prescribed to me as a junior golfer.

Dustin Johnson, one of the top players on the PGA Tour and one of the longest drivers of the golf ball on tour, has extreme lower body rotation in comparison to his shoulders in his downswing and through impact. His belt buckle at impact is already pointing at the target while his shoulders are only slightly open. If he didn't have a strong grip, he would have a very difficult time controlling his golf ball. The more the hips rotate open, the longer the clubface wants to stay open through the strike. The strong grip helps prevent that. It has helped him to win over ten times, place in the top five in five major championships, as well as to be named a member of both the U.S. Ryder Cup and the Presidents Cup teams.

On the opposite side of the spectrum, there is Corey Pavin, a major U.S. Open champion and winner of 28 professional tournaments worldwide, who has a weak grip. Pavin is more of what many would consider an arms swinger—he uses his smaller muscles more in his golf swing and at impact has lower rotation of his lower body compared to his shoulders. Because of that, he has made a modification in how he holds the club (weak grip) so that he can be in control of his clubface through impact. He's known as one of the most accurate drivers ever to play on the PGA Tour.

In order to understand which grip is best for you, we need to first understand your rotational ability. There's an easy way to determine this. First you will need either an impact bag or a duffel bag full of pillows. Place the impact bag up against a firm

Swing at center of impact bag.

Hold club across hips.

surface that won't move easily. Once your station is set up, take a 5-iron stance, and place a golf club on a 45-degree angle running from the toe of your trail foot to the heel of your front foot. You'll use this 45-degree angle to help assist you in testing the rotation of your lower body at impact.

Take your normal grip and address position as if the impact bag is your golf ball. Make a normal swing and strike the center of the impact bag. After you strike the impact bag, I want you to pause, take the club from your hands and place it across your thighs, making sure you maintain your posture as you do. Using the 45-degree angle on the ground, you will able to tell your rotary ability. Do your hips match up with the 45-degree angle or are they in front or behind? Once you successfully measure your angle, you will then know the best way to hold the golf club.

If your hips at impact match up with the 45-degree club on the ground, then your correct grip will be the neutral grip. The neutral grip player should see two knuckles on their lead hand at address while the palm pad sits on top of the grip. The trail hand's thumb pad will then hide most of the lead hand thumb. This will point the crease between the thumb and the index finger of both hands towards the trail ear.

The player whose hips have rotated past the 45-degree mark and are closer to pointing at the target will need a stronger grip. The stronger grip player should be looking for three knuckles on the lead hand with the palm pad still sitting on top of the grip. The crease between the thumb and index finger on the trail hand will then point towards the player's trail shoulder. The other thing this player will have to do is slightly adjust how far he is from the ball at the address position. The higher rotational player will have to stand a touch closer to the ball due to the way their

Neutral grip

Stronger grip

Weak grip

body naturally moves. As the body rotates a greater amount, the golf club moves closer to the body as well, which in a perfect scenario would place the strike more towards the toe of the golf club if the adjustment is not made.

Finally, the golfer whose hips are behind the 45-degree line, or under-rotated, will need to slightly weaken their grip. This player will see two knuckles at address on the lead hand with the palm pad sitting on top of the grip, but the trail hand will be more on top of the lead hand. This places the crease in the trail hand to point vertical and at the player's nose. For more information on how to set up the station and then understand how to prescribe yourself the correct grip, please turn to Your Customized Grip section on page 50.

Years ago, a gentleman by the name of Mike Adam's did great research on the body and golf swing at MIT. I got my idea for this testing based on his research. Mike is one of the top golf coaches in the U.S., and does a lot for coaches and instructors all over the country. I'm happy I had the chance to study his material years ago. It opened up my eyes as a golf coach and has certainly changed how I look at both the golf swing and the player in front of me.

Now that you have your grip synced to your body, we can begin talking about the golf swing itself. There is a certain trait that all of the greats have in common as they begin their backswing and rotate to the top position. This move helps them stabilize and create power with limited wasted motion off of the golf ball. Most golfers I see have a big problem in this particular area. In the next chapter you'll learn what all tour players do that have helped so many of them become household names.

2 TOUR FOUNDATION

The body plays a very important role when swinging the golf club.

I hear comments constantly about how easy the players on the PGA and LPGA Tours make the game of golf look, and they're right! The players on tour show limited motion off the golf ball while making a nice pivot in the backswing. They then begin the downswing with an effortless reaction to the golf ball producing massive power through impact along with impeccable accuracy. They then turn into a nice balanced finish position, which they will hold until the ball lands in close proximity to the target. These players are able to look so graceful because they're swinging with a limited amount of manipulations during their motions. You can do that too!

The second fundamental I've created based on my research is what I call the "Tour Foundation" (Fundamental No. 2). The Tour Foundation is the ability to pivot the hips a specific way in

Proper pelvic motion

Improper pelvic motion

the backswing. This provides a foundation for the torso to move around in the backswing, setting up the rest of the downswing like a chain reaction.

My research has shown that these master players' hips move as if they were inside of a tight barrel. If you were inside this tight barrel, the feeling would be for the trail hip to turn immediately up and back behind, without hitting the side of the barrel. This gets the pelvis turning and tilting with hardly any lateral motion. Research has shown that the tour average of hip sway, or lateral movement in a rotational setting, is approximately three inches towards the target in the backswing based on motion measurement. This places the outside of the trail hip between the instep of the trail foot and the ball of the foot (centered). The trail hip never moves past the center of the trail foot, no matter the club.

Depending on the tour player's age, flexibility, and previous injuries, each shows a different trail knee position to get the hips to move this way. That means that the old adage of keeping the trail knee flexed in the backswing isn't necessarily true based on what the best players in the world are doing. There weren't any patterns when it came to the trail knee position. I found younger players maintaining flexion while others would extend in the backswing (loosing flex to fully straightening). I found the same result for the middle-aged, older, and senior players I studied. This emphasized to me the importance of understanding the body in order to play your best golf game.

No matter the age, weight, height, or flexibility of the golfer, this position is achievable. There will be a few variations in the flexion of the trail knee in the backswing to allow all players to get into the same position. For the younger or more athletic

Three different trailing knee positions

player, the trail knee can maintain its flex, and the player can still make a full shoulder turn while getting the hips to move in a tight circle. For the older or less flexible player, there will be more extending of the trail knee as the shoulders rotate to the top of the backswing.

Before you go any further, please turn to the Tour Foundation section on page 52. You will need to assess your current movement pattern to find the best way you can ingrain the Tour Foundation for yourself. Once you have finished your assessment, come back to this page and continue reading.

If you look at many of the greats of golf—from Sam Snead, Ben Hogan, Arnold Palmer to Jack Nicklaus—you will find that back in their primes none of them maintained flexion in their trail knee in the backswing. In the early '90s, Leadbetter and others began to teach the importance of trail knee stability (maintaining flex) in the backswing. This was the opposite of what the game's greats used to do. Was one player or coach right or wrong? It depends. As a golf coach, I'm only concerned with the golfer in front of me and what that player's capabilities currently are. As I stated earlier, no two golfers are alike; that's why the assessments are extremely important to a player's success.

As a young golf coach years back, I was taught the importance of a flexed trail knee as the upper body coiled around it, creating a stretch factor between the hips and torso in the backswing. The theory was that this stretch factor would create a slingshot-like effect from the top of the backswing, allowing a huge uncoiling of the body, thus providing massive power into impact. I probably hurt more players than I helped. This theory has been proven to be inaccurate. It's been shown that a player who actually has the flexibility to do this (actually very few) can create too much of a stretch, affecting the downswing sequencing of the body, which then causes massive manipulations before impact. When someone with average or limited flexibility attempts this, it's a death move! These players typically move laterally off the golf ball, placing the trail hip outside of the trail foot, which causes the upper body to reverse tilt (spine moving towards the target), resulting in a massive manipulation in the downswing. This has a big effect on the path of the golf club, face orientation, and where the player strikes the ground. These are the issues that 95% of all golfers struggle with today!

It was recently researched and proven that the difference between the average golfer and the tour player—with regard to rotational ability—is fairly close in the backswing when looking at the hip and shoulder rotations and the separation between the two. This goes against much of what is currently taught today. The biggest difference is how the tour player actually begins the downswing compared to the average golfer. The tour players *increase* the separation between the hips and the shoulders, creating that elastic-type power; average players do the complete opposite, which robs them of all their speed and power. The Tour Foundation will help you set up an improved transition in the downswing so that you can begin to produce more elasticity in your downswing.

In the next chapter, we will discuss the third tour fundamental that will get you to transition your body in the downswing, just like the players you watch each week on television. This is one of the most important keys in the golf swing because it has a huge effect on what happens at the moment of impact.

Before you continue, remember: If you find yourself struggling with your contact and overall ball flight, *the first two tour fundamentals are of paramount importance for you and your game.* In Chapter 6, I show you how to test, and then implement, specific drills that you can do both at home and on the range. These drills will teach you to pivot the hips properly while also getting the correct amount of shoulder turn and tilt. The Tour Foundation helps set up the most important part of the golf swing, which you will read about in the following chapter.

3 TOUR TRANSITION

Almost every golfer I've ever come in contact with will ask me one specific question: How do I hit the golf ball farther?

I personally feel all players should be able to pick up some added distance in their game, no matter the level, if they can improve this next position. The position I'm about to discuss is a movement set up by the proper pivoting in the backswing which we looked at in the last chapter on Tour Foundation. Our third tour fundamental will help you use the ground properly as you begin your downswing. I call the third fundamental "Tour Transition" (Fundamental No. 3). This fundamental will help you sequence your body more efficiently, which affects a few key positions in your golf swing to help you hit the ball longer, and achieve your desired ball flight.

In my professional opinion, the first move from the top of the backswing is the most important. This move will set up the rest of the downswing and allow the golfer to either control the golf ball or not. The golf ball doesn't know who you are, but only what you do to it. Through research, I have found that all the players studied have shown a distinct move as they begin the downswing.

The Tour Transition is a move that actually begins *right before* you reach the top of your backswing. As the players are turning the torso around their Tour Foundation (Fundamental No. 2), they reach a point right before the top of the backswing where they all show a lateral bump, or movement towards the target, with their lead hip. The torso is still rotating to an extent, as it's almost in position; and as this is happening, the lower body begins using the ground to move laterally. This move, if done properly, begins to pull the trail shoulder downward as the arms follow, snapping the club in a downward action, causing the club to feel extremely light and in balance. This is how the best players in the world create power. They are using the ground

Tour Transition

properly to help their body function, which is controlling how the golf club is moving.

Over the last few years, technology has been developed that can actually measure how a player is using the ground throughout the golf swing. This technology measures where the pressure in the feet lies as well as how the pressure is traveling during the motion. This technology is called "force plate technology" or "balance plate technology." These highly expensive plate measurements have shown that the better players get the majority of their pressure shifting towards the target from the early stage of the downswing. That is somewhat generalized, as I've learned that each club being hit can cause a slightly different trace but, overall, this is a valid thought process for 99% of golfers out there.

A good visual to help give you an idea of what this may look like would be to imagine a small glass under your lead foot. The tenth of a second before you begin the downswing, your objective is to bump the lead hip forward, and use your force to crush the glass. If this move is done correctly, the majority of the pressure is moving forward and outward. This affects the path on which both the hands and the golf club will travel.

Over the years, many golfers have been given poor or misleading information on how to begin the downswing. The average golfer has been told that the downswing must begin with the hips, which in a sense is correct; unfortunately, most players aren't educated on how to use the hips. What I see in 99.9% of the golfers I work with is a firing of the hips rotary (spinning) from the top of the backswing. Since most golfers have a difficult time separating their lower and upper halves, this is the wrong move. It causes two issues: 1. Low point control (where you strike the

Poor transition

Correct transition

ground) and 2. Swing path issues (the direction the golf club is moving). When a player does this death move, the trail hip and trail shoulder get too high too quickly, causing the swing direction to move drastically inward through impact. Also, the player's weight never gets forward enough. The "death spin," as I call it, is a major reason so many golfers out there tend to slice the golf ball.

In order to get a good feel for what I'm explaining, I suggest you swing the club to the top of the backswing and pause. From this paused position, I want you to keep your shoulders and hips exactly where they are and, without moving the shoulders, just bump your lead hip laterally towards the target. The hips should not rotate or open as you do this. This move, when done correctly, will increase the spine tilt of the upper body, producing a feeling of weight traveling towards the lead foot. The weight should feel as if it's moving towards the ball of the foot (centered) or a touch towards the toes.

In my research, I have found that the average tour player at the delivery position (impact) has about 40 degrees of shoulder tilt (trail shoulder tilting downward). The hip-tilt average (trail hip tilting downward) is only 12 degrees of side bend. The reason for this discrepancy between the two segments has to do with the shoulders providing more forward bend at address opposed to the hips. These numbers for average golfers would decrease due to an improper kinematic sequencing for their personal swing (as mentioned earlier, trail hip and shoulder getting too high in the downswing). This in turn affects a player's swing plane in the downswing leading up to the delivery position at impact.

Many golf instruction books talk about the plane the golf club should move on throughout the swing. Swing plane is determined by two imaginary lines. The primary swing plane is determined by an imaginary line going directly up from the ground, through the shaft, and through the golfer's mid-section until it emerges on the other side of the body. The secondary swing plane line begins at the golf ball and moves directly upwards through the player's trail shoulder from the down-the-line view. These golf instruction books often talk about where they want the club with regard to the swing plane lines, but they never go in-depth on how or what facilitates the swing plane. When it comes to swing plane, I've found that how the body bends, tilts, and turns is what affects the direction of the golf club during the swing.

The biggest issue I commonly see in most golfers is that they get the club too far above or too far below the swing plane in the downswing. The most common is the above-plane swing because these golfers spin the hips from the top of the backswing, which typically causes them to lose side bend or tilt of the hips and shoulders. This causes the trail hip and shoulder to get high (losing body angles) coming down and through impact, which causes the hand path and club head to move drastically in and across through impact. This is why so many golfers in the world struggle with the slice and occasional pull. In this case, you need to feel your back pointing to the target for a longer period as you begin the downswing transitional move that I just mentioned. This will help the trail shoulder to work downwards and out, forcing the hand path and club path to move on an inside-to-out motion into impact. If done correctly, the player will begin to see immediate improvement.

I've found that the better players' miss is a hook or a block, which is the opposite of most golfers; the majority of tour players will tend to fight the same problem. The tour player's miss is also typically a hook or block as that is the miss for a higher caliber player (most of the time).

I always enjoy watching the golf coverage on Sundays because you get to see many of the best players in the world battling, not only their competitors, but also their golf swings as the pressure mounts. When golfers feel uncomfortable, they often begin to do things they wouldn't ordinarily do. For instance, the most common development you will notice on tour is that golfers will begin to walk faster than normal. This begins to have a large effect on their golf game because it increases the heart rate and causes the body to swing the golf club more quickly. Often such players will get very quick in the transition as they begin their downswing, which causes major issues even for the better player. This player's lower body begins moving towards the target well before reaching the top of the backswing. The player gets quick with the lower body, tending to outrace the upper body (rotationally) into impact. This means the golf club can get in a stuck position behind the body, which causes the under-plane swing. Depending on the clubface orientation at impact, this will produce the block or the dreaded snap hook.

In 2000, Tiger Woods was statistically the second-longest hitter on tour. He was 54th in overall accuracy, hitting 71% of his fairways. Being long and accurate was certainly one of Tiger's strengths when he was dominating the tour. As he's gotten older and he continues to make more changes to his once-technically-perfect golf swing, he has slowly fallen farther and farther in both the driving-distance and driving-accuracy categories. In both 2013 and 2014, he dropped to 49th in driving distance on tour, and became 69th in driving accuracy—hitting just 62% of his fairways. He has also become more injury-prone over the last few years. Age is a factor here; nevertheless, I studied his swing from 2000 to 2011, and then compared that to his 2012 to 2014 swing where he began to have more issues with the driver and with his back, and discovered a few nuggets that supported my research.

In 2000, Tiger Woods showed all of the 5 Tour Fundamentals that I've found but, most importantly, he transitioned nicely at Fundamental No. 3, allowing the shoulders to tilt and turn correctly, providing an improved position at No. 4, which we will get into in the next chapter. This proper positioning of the hands at impact allows for the clubface and path to match up in an effective fashion, so that he could predict his ball flight much more often.

In 2012 to 2014, I noticed Tiger beginning to have issues with fundamentals number three and four, which caused the lower and upper body to work improperly. This produced too much tilting of the shoulders, causing him to get narrow into impact, while providing too much shaft lean, thus placing the hand position too far in front of the lead thigh. This was most pronounced in his driver swing.

When a golfer gets narrow in the downswing, it often means there is too much lagging of the club. This means that the hands get very close to the body, as the shaft is still vertical, causing the player to then make a major manipulation right before impact in order to get the clubhead on the ball. This causes a reverse-C position before impact: The upper body is pulling back and up as the lower body is trying to move forward. This was the biggest reason Tiger had issues at the impact position with his driver, and also a major reason he began to experience back injuries.

If you can improve your Tour Foundation in the backswing, it will have a huge impact on the transitional move we just discussed in this chapter. You will be amazed at the power and stability you will feel once you master the Tour Transition. You are getting one step closer to lowering your handicap, and potentially shooting that career-low round! Next we will talk about my discovery regarding the impact position or, as I like to call it, the delivery position.

4 TOUR DELIVERANCE

As I searched through my database of touring professionals, I found only two things each professional did the same at the moment of the strike.

The first thing shouldn't be much of a surprise to most players: The first item I found each professional did was strike the golf ball first. I know you're probably thinking, "Wow, that's groundbreaking information there, Bill!" But it's true. That's the only thing they all do alike, other than the next very important key I'm about to discuss: The impact position, or as I've coined it for our fourth tour fundamental "Tour Deliverance" (Fundamental No. 4).

The impact position is one of the most important—if not *the* most important—position in the golf swing. The impact position is set up based on what the golfer does throughout the golf swing leading up to the moment of the strike. Impact is often called "the moment of truth" because everything a player does in the pre-swing, backswing, and downswing sets up this delivery position.

In the course of my research, I came across an interesting find as I studied swing after swing. I found that no matter which club is being hit, the hand position at the moment of impact is always the same. This is a pretty interesting find when you think about all the different golf swings on tour, added to the fact that all players are different shapes and sizes and show varying levels of athleticism.

There are many things that golf coaches look for at the moment of impact. You will hear many coaches say that, at impact, one must maintain the body angle, have a certain amount of body rotation, hit into a firm lead side, and provide lower-body stability through the strike. What I have found from studying today's best players is that they don't necessarily show all of these. In fact, many don't show half! My goal in writing this book is to point out proven keys that golfers can apply to their game. Since all golfers are different, not every player will be able to achieve what many will ask of them. The good news is, all will be able to achieve Fundamental No. 4.

The fourth fundamental, Tour Deliverance, is all about the deliverance of the hands into the hitting area. The path the hands travel on, and their position with regard to the body, is extremely important when it comes to producing a reliable ball flight. All players I researched delivered their hand position in front of the lead thigh at impact, no matter the club or ball position. This ensures that the shorter clubs will have more shaft lean due to the ball position being centered to back of the stance, as the club lengthens the ball position moving forward. This produces less shaft lean until the player gets to the driver, which should show

Proper impact position

With differing ball positions

Club Awareness Drill

very little lean or no lean at all. No matter the club being hit, the positioning of the hands will remain the same. Hand positioning in regards to the lead thigh stays the same, but shaft lean changes due to the ball position depending on the club being hit.

A great drill to help achieve this deliverance position is one that was shown to me by Gary Gilchrist. He learned this particular drill from David Leadbetter during his time at the Leadbetter Academy years ago. Gary uses this drill for different positions throughout the golf swing, but I love what it can do for the player's impact position. He called this drill "Club Awareness."

Begin by taking your address position, choking down on the club, and allowing the hands to be placed halfway between the grip and the clubhead. This allows the shaft to run up against the lead hip. From this position, you keep the club on the hip until the hands pass the trail knee; the hands and body then continue to pivot, hinging the club upwards, which takes it off of the hip until the top of the backswing is completed. You then begin the downswing, delivering the shaft back onto the lead hip into the delivery position (impact). This places the hands in the correct position. You can try this with a 9-iron all the way up to a driver. Vary where the ball position will be, i.e., try the 9-iron slightly back of center, all the way to the driver being off the lead instep. You will find that the shaft lean changes, but the hand position never does.

The 2014 PGA Tour season saw Tiger Woods out for months due to a back injury. When he was able to play, he was playing with a two-way miss off the tee. This was causing very poor driving statistics. The biggest reason Tiger had issues with his back, and his overall driving, was due to the way his body moved in the downswing. This was causing an improper hand position at impact with the longer clubs. In my opinion, Tiger's back problems began due to an improper motor pattern, which increased his spine angle in the downswing. This caused his hands to be too far out in front of his forward thigh with the driver. It also increased pressure in the lumbar spine, making it nearly impossible to control his tee shots.

In my research, I compared his 2012 to 2014 golf swing with his golf swings from 2000. In the year 2000, Tiger was unbeatable. He won six events in a row, totaling nine for the season. He broke the PGA Tour's scoring average record, and won a U.S. Open, which gave him the career Grand Slam—and he won that U.S. Open by 15 shots!

When comparing the two swings, which were now 14 years apart, I found that in 2000, Tiger fell into all five tour fundamentals I discovered. In 2014, he did not, and he definitely was missing the boat in the deliverance position at impact with the driver. There wouldn't be many players who would be able to play without injuries by putting themselves in the same positions in the downswing.

On the opposite side of the spectrum, players like Ben Hogan, Matt Kuchar, and Lee Westwood have all pulled themselves out of massive—almost career-ending—slumps by making changes to their games that fit into my 5 Tour Fundamentals. Ben Hogan couldn't control his ball flight at a certain point in his career, which almost made him quit the game. Instead, he decided to make massive changes in his grip, from strong to weak, and he changed how he used his trail knee to (in his own words) "initiate the swing," which allowed him to perform Fundamental No. 2. These two changes, which are found in *The 5 Tour Fundamentals of Golf*, allowed him to resurrect his career and eventually win 64 tour events including the Grand Slam!

Matt Kuchar was a star golfer. As an amateur golfer, he won a U.S. Amateur, and was a standout golfer for Georgia Tech. The U.S. Amateur win got him into the Masters as an amateur, in which he finished in the top 15. This was unheard of at the time. He later turned pro, but struggled for quite some time. He was forced to either make a swing change or his career would be over. He and his coach developed a way he could best swing the golf club based on what his body wanted to do naturally. The changes he made allowed him to become one of the best ball strikers on the PGA Tour. Since that time, he has won seven tournaments and played on multiple Ryder Cup and Presidents Cup teams representing the U.S.

Finally, Lee Westwood, who seems to be on almost every leaderboard today, almost gave up the game due to a career

Poor hand position (too much lean)

Poor hand position (cupped wrists)

Proper tour hand position

slump. In 2000, he became the fourth-best golfer in the world. Two years later, he dropped out of the top 300 in the world! In 2003, he finally got his career back on track by making changes that eventually would match up with my research, thus putting him in The 5 Tour Fundamentals category.

If you can conquer the first four tour fundamentals, you will be able to control the circumference of your golf swing at impact, providing an improved delivery position of the hands. This will allow you to hit the golf ball first, while also having control over the clubface as well as over the direction the club path is moving.

In order to get a better understanding of the deliverance position, please turn to page 63. In this section, you will find both indoor and outdoor drills to help you consistently achieve the positions used by the best players in the world.

5 TOUR STRETCH

You are now just one step away from learning the last key, which all touring professionals have in common.

So far, you've discovered the first four of my five tour fundamentals. I'm hoping I've provided you with a good understanding of:

1. The correct grip for you
2. Pivoting your pelvis in the backswing
3. Transitioning correctly in order to set up the downswing
4. The proper delivery position of your hands at impact

These four fundamentals were all found in the professional golfers I researched for this project. Our final fundamental is no different. This fifth fundamental found in my research is what I call the "Tour Stretch" (Fundamental No. 5). The Tour Stretch happens after the strike, but is just as important as the other four fundamentals listed in this book.

The order in which the body functions and fires throughout the golf swing is paramount in setting up the fifth and final tour fundamental. Some may ask why a position *after* the strike is important since the ball has already been struck. It's important because it shows the effect of the rest of the golf swing prior to impact. The way the body is able to go from flexion (forward bend) into extension (losing forward bend) throughout impact as the player rotates into the through-swing, is universal in the players I've studied. This movement provides a certain positioning of the trail arm from post-impact until the arm is past parallel to the ground.

Every player I studied showed the trail arm straightening just after impact until the arm was at least parallel to the ground. This positioning creates width between the hands and body as the player rotates. While the player is rotating, and the trail arm is becoming closer to parallel with the ground, the body is extending (losing forward bend) as the player rotates into a nicely balanced finish position.

Many golfers I see have issues beginning early in the downswing. Most of the time, it's because of an issue with the player's backswing. This has a large effect on the player's body pivot and hand path, which causes an issue with the club path and clubface. The average golfer typically has a transition issue at the beginning of the downswing, causing the hand path to move inward, which pulls the club with it. This player doesn't have any extension after impact and into Fundamental No. 5, Tour Stretch. Instead, the elbows quickly increase their bend after impact, causing the lead arm to bend away from the body as the trail arm folds into the body. This causes what many of us call the dreaded "chicken wing." This position got its name based on the view from behind the golfer: The lead elbow points outward, looking like a wing. Ideally, the lead elbow should extend and then fold up against the body after impact as the player continues to rotate into the finish position. Golfers who find themselves in the chicken wing position typically are slicers of the golf ball, and they have limited power.

Drills in the Tour Stretch section on page 66 will give you the best visual of what the tour extension position should look like. These drills show how you can practice the position both off the golf ball as well as on the golf ball. Please turn to pages 68 to 71 and review the Extension and Railroad Drills. The Extension Drill should be done inside in the comfort of your home. This drill will begin to train your body how it should move and extend without the need of the golf club. The Extension Drill will eventually lead you into the Railroad Drill, which is the full-swing version of the previous drill with a golf club in hand. These drills will provide you with the correct stretch and extension found in the best players in the world.

The better golfers are often challenged when they get their clubs working too far behind their bodies in the downswing due to a poor Fundamental No. 3, which gets them into a stuck position. This causes the swing direction to move well outward through impact, causing the arms to extend and get separated from the body. These players' miss is a block or snap hook, depending on the face orientation and centeredness of contact through impact. The body, at times, outraces the player's arms and hands leaving those arms and hands "deeper" or too far behind them in the downswing. This will have a big effect on the path of both the hands and the club, which has an influence on the clubface angle at impact. This movement also will have an effect on where the

Poor extension (chicken wing)

Poor extension (disconnect)

Correct tour stretch

golfer is striking the ball of the clubface at impact. This player's arms will then get "disconnected" or move in the opposite direction of where the body is rotating after impact and into the extension position.

In this case, you need to feel as if you are trying to shake hands with someone when the club is parallel to the ground in the through swing (after impact). If you can "shake hands" with the target when the trail arm is parallel to the ground in the through swing, it will ensure that the arms are working with the body. You don't want the trail forearm and hand pointing too far upwards or downwards at this point.

In my research and experience watching high-level amateurs and professionals, I have yet to see a great player have a poor Tour Stretch. This fundamental says a lot about the player's golf swing. If you can consistently get into the correct position here, it shows that you did great things during the rest of your golf swing setting up this position.

I've always been interested in understanding the reason something works. If you can't prove it to me, I will typically be pretty skeptical. As the years have gone by in my coaching career, I've at times found it frustrating that golf instruction information isn't always factually accurate. I think of a golf lesson like a doctor's appointment: When I go to the doctor, I want a factual diagnosis on how I can begin to feel better. Golf should be no different.

The positions discussed in this book have a large effect on almost everything imaginable in your golf swing. To keep it simple, I decided it would be best if I didn't mention all of the parts of your swing affected. With that being said, please believe me: If you can master The 5 Tour Fundamentals of Golf, you will begin to master your golf game! I truly believe that if you can take time out of your schedule to work on these five areas, you will lower your score more quickly than you ever have before. In order to help you with the improvement process, I have added drills and tests that you can work on—both at home and on the range. The training process is obviously important, but remember: Training doesn't need to take a long time if you train smart!

The drills in the following chapter will allow you to train wisely and efficiently both at home and at the course.

6 TRAIN SMART

The key to making lasting changes in a golf swing begins with the ability to train smart.

If done correctly, proper training techniques will allow you to make lasting changes in your game. Unfortunately, most golfers don't know how to train or practice effectively. That is why so many golfers never improve. They don't have a game plan in place to help their overall progress as a golfer.

I have developed a systematic way of training that all golfers should adhere to if they want to improve. The great thing about my training program is, it can be accomplished in a limited amount of time. The saying "Less is more" applies here if you do the drills correctly and on a consistent basis over a specific period of time.

In this chapter, you will find my technical training model to help you obtain The 5 Tour Fundamentals of Golf. The training is made up of both indoor and outdoor drills. With a combination of the two, you will be able to change your motor patterns more quickly, which will allow you to improve more rapidly. Since we are only concerned with changing your current motor patterns, don't get caught up in the overall outcome while training. This time should be taken to slowly remove the old patterns and ingrain the new.

During this time, you should be working on drills specific to the need to help the improvement process. How you use your time to work on these drills is very valuable. As I stated earlier, less is more, so if you are training and working on the drills correctly for 30 minutes, you will get much more out of it than if you were to hit balls for hours at a time playing the guessing game.

The five fundamentals are made up of tests and drills to help you understand your ability, and to implement the correct changes based on that understanding. Each drill listed will give you a time frame for that period of training.

Training mirror

The first three fundamentals should be emphasized with maximum importance during the first few weeks of your training. These fundamentals will help you achieve the last two of the five tour fundamentals. In the following pages, you will find tests and drills for each chapter. In each area, there will be a specific number of reps you will need to do for each drill in order to begin to change your current pattern.

Fundamental No. 1: Grip Sync

Impact Bag Test

To properly assess yourself during this first test, you will need to find an impact bag. If you don't have an impact bag, you can create one by using a duffel bag filled with clothes or pillows. Once you have your impact bag, find a firm surface on which to rest the

Impact Bag Test

bag. Place a golf club on a 45-degree angle, as we did in the first chapter. Make sure this club runs from the inside of the trail toe down to the inside of the lead heel. Address the impact bag and make a normal swing, striking the center of the bag. After you have struck the bag, hold that position and place the club on your thighs. Are they rotated past 45 degrees? Are the hips at a perfect 45-degree angle? Or are the hips rotated less than the 45-degree mark? This will help you understand the correct grip to sync to your body.

Next I will explain the correct grip based on your testing. The one disclaimer I have to offer when talking about the different grips below is the importance of the base of the player's palm pad in the lead hand. No matter the grip, this pad should always sit on top of the grip. This is important in order to help you hinge the club properly in the backswing, control the clubface, and release and extend just after the moment of impact.

Your Customized Grip

If your hips are out in front of the 45-degree line created by the shaft on the ground, causing your belt buckle to point more

Higher rotational ability, strong grip

towards the target at impact, you have higher rotational ability. This rotational ability calls for a stronger grip because when the hips continue to rotate to the extent you're experiencing, the closure of the clubface takes a longer amount of time. This means the clubface will tend to stay more open. The stronger grip will help.

If the hips match up with the 45-degree shaft on the ground, you have standard rotational ability. This standard ability calls for the neutral-grip position. This is the grip that's prescribed in almost every golf instruction book ever written. Typically, with standard rotational players, the hips and shoulders will match

Standard rotational ability, neutral grip

up nicely at impact, which is why the neutral grip is the proper connection in this case.

If the hips are just slightly open after striking the bag and haven't reached the angle of the 45-degree mark, you will be classified as a lower-rotational-ability player. Therefore, you're typically more of an arms swinger, meaning you will have a tendency to shut the clubface with your hands through impact. A slightly weaker grip will hold the face open for a longer period of

Lower rotational ability, weaker grip

time, preventing rapid closure of the clubhead. If you are this type of player, typically you aren't able to create the same power source with your body as the standard- or higher-rotational player does, so you'll make up for it by using smaller muscles. Knowing this, the proper grip for the lower-rotational player is the weaker grip. This will help you improve your clubface angle at impact.

Now that you have chosen the correct grip for your rotational ability, you will learn how to test your lower-body flexibility for Fundamental No. 2. This is a key point to help you achieve the Tour Foundation at the top of the backswing. Once you understand your range of motion, you can then move on to the drills. These drills will provide the feedback necessary to obtain the correct trail hip position at the top of the backswing.

Fundamental No. 2: Tour Foundation

45-Degree Angle Drill

In order to get the lower body to achieve the Tour Foundation, we must first understand your range of motion with the lower body. The best drill to determine this is the 45-Degree Angle Drill. The test begins by placing one club on a 45-degree angle running from the inside of your lead toe down through the inside of your trail heel. You should be in a 5-iron address position when performing this drill.

Begin by placing a golf club on your shoulders at the address position. Make your normal backswing pivot, and pause once you reach the top of your backswing. From this position, take

45-Degree Angle Drill

the club from your shoulders and place it on the upper thighs without moving the body. You can see what your natural lower-body rotation is by looking at the 45-degree alignment stick on the ground. Ideally, it should match the angle on the ground as the trail hip is moving up and back. If you come up short of the 45-degree mark, lose a bit of flexion in the trail knee as the lower body pivots, which will allow the hips to increase rotation.

If you find the shaft on the thighs goes past the 45-degree mark, first make sure the trail hip is actually moving up and behind, and not laterally. If it's moving up and behind, you will need to kick the trail knee towards the target a touch at the address position, placing more weight on the instep and allowing more stability in the knee. This will increase flexion in the knee and allow the hips to match up to the 45-degree shaft on the ground.

Loss of flexion in trail knee

Increased flexion of the knee

Tour Foundation Pivot Drill

This is a great drill to familiarize your lower body with movements that help build your Tour Foundation. You won't need a golf club, but you will need a table or desk to help assist you with this indoor drill.

Correct

Correct

Incorrect

Tour Foundation Pivot Drill

Take a 5-iron address position with your trail leg approximately two inches from the table. Cross your arms, placing your hands on your shoulders. Add a slight tilt of the torso away from where the target would be. This tilt will simulate your normal address position, as if you were holding a club. You will now make a backswing pivot. You should feel the trail hip actually getting farther away from the desk as you rotate your torso to the top of the backswing. The trail hip should not move towards the tabletop at any time; it should move upwards and back.

Training: This drill should be done for five minutes, four nights a week for the first few weeks until you feel you can achieve the position correctly while training. If possible, use a mirror to give you a visual of how your body is moving. After the first few weeks, monitor it closely. You can then begin to drop to two nights per week. This will allow you to build in positive reps.

This indoor drill is something that should be maintained over a long period of time, as it's extremely important in assisting the transition to set up the downswing.

Alignment Stick Drill

The alignment stick drill gives immediate feedback as to where the hips are pivoting in the backswing. You will first need to find an alignment stick or snow stick. These can be found at any hardware store.

Place the alignment stick in the ground on a slight angle to match up with the angle of your front leg at the address position. As you begin your backswing, you will get the trail hip to move both up and back behind you. If you do this correctly, you will

Correct

Correct

Incorrect

Alignment Stick Drill

feel the alignment stick touching the back upper portion of your lead leg. This drill will overemphasize the position, which is what needs to be done at first in order to change the motor pattern. The drill will ensure that your hips are pivoting as if inside a tight barrel. Use the photos as your reference point for what this position should look like.

Training: Train using this drill two times a week while training outdoors, four reps of eight balls each. The indoor version of this drill will make this outdoor drill much easier if you can stick to the game plan. When training, do one rep (eight balls) using the drill; then take the alignment stick away, and hit another eight balls with a normal swing. Then for the next rep, bring the alignment stick back in and repeat.

Training using the total amount of reps, with and without the alignment stick, should take under 30 minutes of your time. If you want to improve, take 30 minutes out of your schedule—only two days a week—to perform this very important drill.

You now have the correct pre-swing and backswing fundamentals as demonstrated by today's best players. It's now time to improve your downswing. Fundamental No. 3, Tour Transition, is essential in setting up the path the golf club will travel in the downswing. This first move from the top of the backswing controls the angles of the body, ensuring an on-plane downswing.

In the following pages, you will find two drills to help you achieve the proper transition displayed by the best players on the planet. The first drill can easily be done in the comfort of your own home. I suggest beginning with this drill to effectively change your current motor pattern. Doing this drill without a golf club will help you achieve an improved transition quicker once you get to the practice facility.

Fundamental No. 3: Tour Transition

Indoor Pivot Bump Test

Using the same desk or table used previously, you will set up with the lead leg approximately two inches from the table. There is no need for a golf club while doing this drill (the photos on the following page show the same drill with a golf club).

As prescribed in Fundamental No. 2, cross your arms, placing your hands on your shoulders. Then tilt the spine slightly away from the target to simulate the setup position as if you were gripping the club. Now pivot to the top of your backswing using the Tour Foundation move you just learned. Once you reach the top of the backswing, you will pause. From here, you will bump your hips towards the desk or table without rotating your hips or torso. This will be a lateral motion using only the hips.

If you're doing it properly, you should be able to bump the hips into the object. You will begin to feel the weight shifting towards the lead leg as the shoulders stay in place and maintain the spine angle. This will ensure the correct transition to get the club moving correctly in the downswing.

Training: Do this three days a week at home for five minutes at a time. This drill needs to be done diligently for one month. Once you begin to see improvements after the first month, you can scale back.

Correct Indoor Pivot Bump Test *Incorrect*

As I noted in the section for Fundamental No. 2, these indoor drills are very important for your improvement. They will begin to change your current motor pattern, and help you immensely once you train using the outdoor version of the drill.

Alignment Stick Bump Pivot Drill

This alignment stick drill is the outdoor version of the previous drill. First, take an alignment stick or snow stick and place it in the ground. Take your address position, placing the lead foot up

Alignment Stick Bump Pivot Drill

against the stick. This stick should be vertical and centered on the outside of the lead foot. From here, you will swing to the top of the backswing and pause. You should then bump the hips, as you have been doing using the indoor version of this drill.

If done properly, without rotation, you should feel the stick on the back of your lead leg. From there, you can then swing the arms downward as the body rotates, and strike the ball. This is a drill to overemphasize the transitional move. Use the photos as a visual to ensure that you do the drill properly.

Training: Train using this drill two times a week outdoors, consisting of four reps of eight balls each. Begin with the drill, then hit eight balls with a normal swing, then go back to the drill for your second rep, and repeat. Train this way until you reach your four reps. Train using the total amount of reps with and without the alignment stick.

This should take under 30 minutes of your time. If you're dedicated, you should be able to take 30 minutes out of your schedule for only two days a week to perform this very important drill.

You have now started to improve your transition, which will help set up the rest of your downswing. Your new transition will help improve the plane of the downswing, the clubface-path relationship, the impact position, and you'll also see increased power. As discussed earlier, the first three fundamentals are essential in order to perfect fundamentals four and five. The golf swing is just one big chain reaction, and each position has an effect on the next. If one link is out of sync, it will derail the operation.

The remaining drills should not begin until four weeks into your training. You should concentrate your efforts on the first three fundamentals, as they will help facilitate the remaining positions—Tour Deliverance and Tour Extension—of The 5 Tour Fundamentals of Golf. The following drills will help improve your tour deliverance position by providing you with the correct feel of the positioning of the hands at impact.

Fundamental No. 4: Tour Deliverance

Club Awareness Drill

This is a great drill to do in the comfort of your own home. This is one of my favorite drills to help change a player's motor patterns, while helping improve the tour deliverance position (impact).

Club Awareness Drill

Begin by choking halfway down on a 5-iron. The hands should be touching the steel or graphite of the club shaft. As you're doing this, the shaft should run up the lead side and sit flush against your lead hip. From this address position, slowly pivot, keeping the shaft on the hip for the first few inches in the takeaway, until the hands pass the trail knee in the backswing. It will then leave the hip and hinge upwards as you reach the top of the backswing.

During this time, you should be feeling your new Tour Foundation in the backswing. As you reach the top of the backswing and begin the downswing, you will slowly deliver the club back into impact, allowing the shaft to sit flush against your lead hip again. Make sure you pause at the delivery position. This will put your hand position in the perfect deliverance position, no matter the club being hit. This will also place your hands centered in front of the lead thigh, no matter the club being swung. As you get better at this drill, you can begin to gradually speed up your tempo.

> **Training:** After four weeks into your training, you can apply this drill three times a week, with each rep lasting five minutes.
>
> The first month is extremely important for developing the first three fundamentals. These fundamentals will help set up the last two remaining positions.

Whoosh Drill

You can do this drill while you're training on the range, using any club. Work on this drill in between sessions, back behind the golf ball. Begin by making practice swings using your normal tempo in the backswing and downswing. Then attempt to

Whoosh Drill

immediately freeze at the delivery position (impact). You should be able to stop at impact, allowing your hands to be centered off the lead thigh. Your hands should never end up in front or behind the thigh; this would be poor deliverance. This drill will also develop core strength over time, which can eventually help the body function more efficiently.

Training: This outdoor drill should consist of three reps at eight swings each. Do the first set; then hit eight balls full-swing; then begin the second set and repeat the process.

These drills will give you the correct sensation of where hand placement should be at the impact position. The only thing you need to be conscious of after performing these drills is making sure the ball is in the appropriate position for the club to be hit. Depending on your desired ball flight and trajectory, the ball position can be slightly different for each club, whether you want to see a draw or a fade. I prefer all players to begin with the ball positioning I'm about to explain.

For the shorter irons—wedges, 9-, and 8-irons—I like the ball position to be off the player's nose or more centered. For the 7-, 6-, and 5-irons, I like the ball position to be off the forward ear or slightly forward of center. As the clubs get longer—4-, 3-, hybrids, fairway woods, and even drivers—the ball position creeps forward until it's off of the lead instep of the forward foot. If you like to see the ball draw, you can move the ball positioning slightly back of what I suggested, but by only about one golf ball. If you prefer to see the ball fade, do the opposite. You should move the ball a touch forward in your swing, but again by only one golf ball.

Fundamental No. 5:
Tour Stretch

This final tour fundamental will show how well you did at achieving the first four fundamentals. The first four fundamentals dictate whether you will be able to achieve the fifth and final tour fundamental. In other words, everything done in the pre-swing,

Up and Under Drill

backswing, and downswing will make the tour stretch position achievable or not. Below are a few drills to give you the correct sensation for what the Tour Stretch should look and feel like post impact.

Under and Up Drill

This drill is my favorite for helping you shallow the golf club in order to improve your swing plane. This drill will allow for an improved Tour Stretch as well.

Begin by taking your address position with the club upside-down in your trail arm only. From this position, place your lead arm in a straight-out position, parallel to the ground, placing it just above the belt line. Swing the club back halfway and through with the trail arm only, allowing the club to stay underneath the forward arm that's extended. The forward arm stays extended the entire time and should have minimal movement. This means the shoulders stay relatively square as the trail arm swings underneath, extends, and then goes upward towards your lead shoulder. The hips will rotate, but the shoulders will have minimal movement. This provides the correct amount of side-bend at impact, and then allows the body to extend correctly as the player reaches the Tour Stretch position.

Training: I suggest five drills for each ball hit over a 15-minute period during outdoor training. This is a great drill to give you the correct feel of the tour stretch. As directed earlier, this drill should not begin until you feel you are able to improve the first three fundamentals, as those will help facilitate the Tour Stretch position.

Extension Drill

The Extension Drill is a great drill you can do without a golf club. It will teach you the correct motor pattern of how the trail elbow works in the backswing and impact and then, most importantly, into the Tour Stretch.

You need to find a wall in order to do this drill. First, stand a few inches away from the wall, as shown in the photos. Begin with the trail arm extended and relaxed at address. As you begin the backswing, the trail elbow will bend as it would in

Extension Drill

the golf swing. You should stop once the upper portion of the trail arm is parallel to the ground. From this position, begin the downswing, stopping at impact. At impact, the trail arm will have a slight amount of bend. This is what the best players in the world do. From the impact position, extend the arm down the target line as you rotate, and eventually your hand will strike the wall. When the hand strikes the wall, the arm should still be extended, and the entire palm of the hand should sit flush against the wall. This simulates the proper clubface at this point in the golf swing.

Training: This drill should be done two times per week, each session lasting five minutes. This is a good drill to work on in the comfort of your own home. It will give you a great sense of what the body should be doing, without the use of a golf club.

Railroad Drill

This drill will give you the correct visual on what the club and body should be doing just after impact, which will allow for the correct Tour Stretch position.

You will need two golf clubs or two alignment sticks for this drill. You will set up one alignment stick approximately five feet in front of the ball on the target line. You will then take the second alignment stick and place it about two feet to the inside of the first. The second alignment stick should be square with the center of the foot. You've now created "railroad tracks"—hence the name! In order for the best possible chance to achieve Tour Stretch, you must put yourself to my first five fundamentals.

Railroad Drill

This drill will give you a great visual on what happens prior to impact, and how that has a great effect on the post-impact positioning of the Tour Stretch. Like many drills, this drill will overemphasize the stretch that happens after impact and into the through swing.

First, make a three-quarter backswing, then slowly begin the downswing as you reach impact. You should feel as if you are trying to extend the clubhead down the line, which sits five feet in front of where the ball lay originally. As the body continues to turn and the club becomes parallel to the ground in the through swing, the club should match the inside track. As you continue to rotate even further, the trail arm will then match the inside track as the golf club works upwards. You should be able to stop once you get to this position. This will give you a dynamic move, helping you to improve swing direction as well as the movement and extension of the body.

Training: This drill should be mixed in while working on the previous drill. The drill is made up of three reps of eight swings while training outdoors. This drill should only take about 15 to 20 minutes, allowing you to improve without spending hours at the range.

The five tour fundamentals listed in this book are obtainable by any and all golfers. All you have to do is stick to the detailed plan that I've listed in this chapter. This regimen does not need to take a long period of time. In fact, a few minutes nightly can go a long way—without having to hit a golf ball. Early in the training process, you are attempting to change a current motor pattern. The way to change an old pattern is to ingrain a new one into your daily routine.

The easiest way to stick to a daily and weekly schedule is to write each week out on paper or on a whiteboard. You want to make sure that you are holding yourself accountable every day!

The players I've had the most success with throughout my career have always been able to develop and follow a daily or weekly routine. These players are also smart about how they train. They train for short periods of time, working only on what's listed in the game plan. There is no need to spend hours hitting golf balls in order to improve and lower your score. In fact, more often than not, that can be the *worst* thing for a player to do.

Follow all of the drills in this chapter, and you'll see that you can improve, no matter how busy you may be. This is training smart!

ABOUT THE AUTHOR

BILL SCHMEDES III is an American PGA golf coach, player development specialist, and golf swing researcher. He is recognized by many of his peers as one of the top up-and-coming golf coaches in the country. He has been recognized by the PGA and various major publications for his abilities as a golf instructor and coach.

Bill began his professional career on Cape Cod, Massachusetts after finishing his collegiate golf career at Thomas College where he was recognized as a NCAA NAC First Team All-Conference player. After turning professional, he quickly got his feet wet by becoming the Assistant Golf Professional at Blue Rock Golf Club, a Cape Cod resort and site of the largest golf academy in the area. This is where Bill first discovered his love for golf instruction.

A few years later, Bill moved on to become a full-time golf coach working at GolfTEC in Cranston, Rhode Island. He became intrigued with the technological advancements in the golf industry, and used that technology to help his players improve more quickly. The technologies included motion measurement and 3D Doppler, which chart how the body moves as well as the movement of the golf club.

He was offered a position working with Gary Gilchrist in Orlando, Florida, and assisted Gary with his players on the PGA, European, LPGA, and Web.com tours. He also became a head coach for Gilchrist's junior golf academy, which allowed him to work with many of the top players in the world.

Over the years, Bill has had the opportunity to work with over twelve touring professionals. These players include major champions, USA Presidents Cup players, U.S. and European Solheim Cup team members, and the former number one women's golfer in the world. He has given lessons to various celebrities and many of the top juniors in the world of golf. Bill has been named a Top 25 Golf Instructor in New England, nominated for PGA Teacher of the Year in two different sections and chapters. He was recently nominated by *Golf Digest* for its "Best Young Teachers in America" list.

Bill is currently Director of Instruction at Fiddler's Elbow Country Club in Bedminster, New Jersey. Fiddler's Elbow is the largest private golf facility in New Jersey, boasting over 54 holes of golf and a state-of-the-art learning center.

For additional information or
to contact Bill Schmedes III, visit:
http://www.bs3golf.com/

CPSIA information can be obtained at www.ICGtesting.com
Printed in the USA
BVOW02s2120240315

393184BV00002B/2/P

9 780990 763123